Bees

Aaron Frisch

CREATIVE EDUCATION

seedlings

Published by Creative Education
P.O. Box 227, Mankato, Minnesota 56002
Creative Education is an imprint of
The Creative Company
www.thecreativecompany.us

Design and production by Ellen Huber
Art direction by Rita Marshall
Printed in the United States of America

Photographs by Alamy (WILDLIFE GmbH), Corbis (Fritz
Rauschenbach), Dreamstime (PeterWaters), Getty Images (Ingo
Arndt, Heidi & Hans-Jurgen Koch, Thomas Lottermoser, Sylvia
Cook Photography, Visuals Unlimited, Inc./Eric Tourneret),
Shutterstock (12_Tribes, Alekcey, Geanina Bechea, irin-k,
kesipun, PCHT, sergey23, Craig Taylor, tr3gin, Peter Waters),
SuperStock (Minden Pictures)

Library of Congress Cataloging-in-Publication Data
Frisch, Aaron.
Bees / Aaron Frisch.
p. cm. — (Seedlings)
Includes bibliographical references and index.
Summary: A kindergarten-level introduction to bees, covering
their growth process, behaviors, the hives they call home, and
such defining physical features as their stingers.
ISBN 978-1-60818-456-9
1. Bees—Juvenile literature. I. Title.

QL568.A6F598 2014
595.79'9—dc23   2013029062

CCSS: RI.K.1, 2, 3, 4, 5, 6, 7;
RI.1.1, 2, 3, 4, 5, 6, 7; RF.K.1, 3; RF.1.1

First Edition
9 8 7 6 5 4 3 2 1

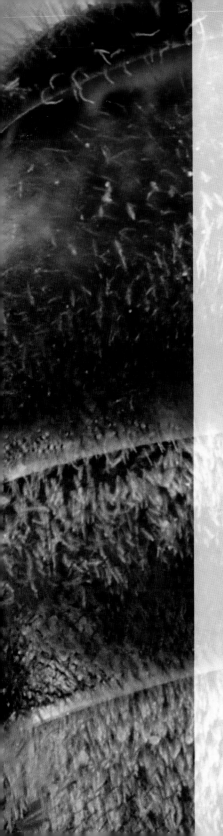
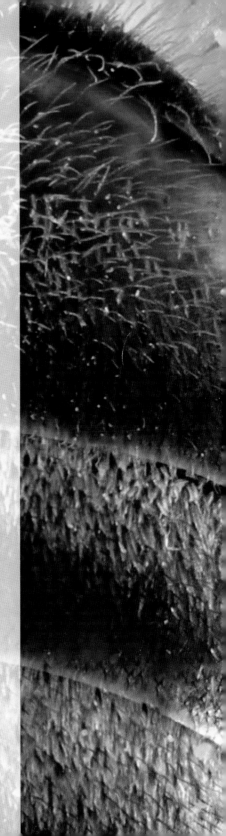

TABLE OF CONTENTS

Hello, bees!

Bees are bugs that fly.

They make a buzzing sound.

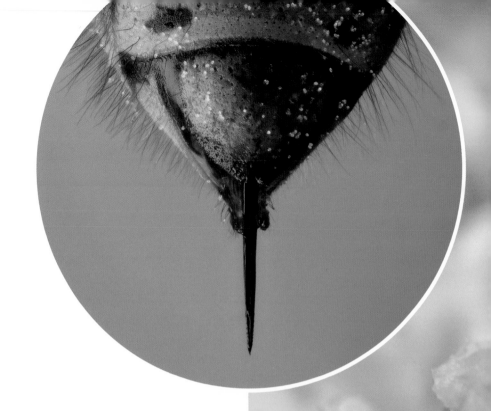

Bees have striped bodies. They have one pair of wings. Some bees have sharp stingers.

9

Bees live in big groups.
They build nests in trees or rocks.

A bee nest is
called a hive.

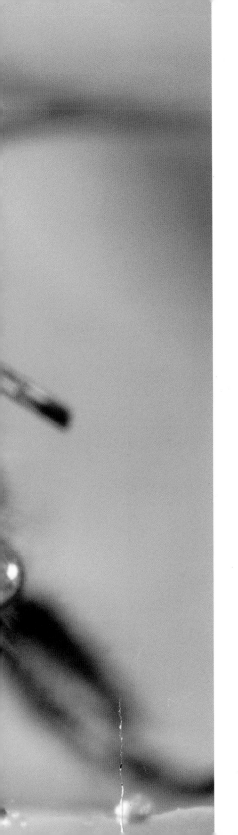

Bees pick up pollen and nectar from flowers. They make nectar into honey.

A baby bee
comes out
of an egg.
First it looks
like a worm.

But it grows quickly!

Bees fly around
to find food.
They keep the
hive clean. They
feed baby bees.

17

Goodbye, bees!

Picture a Bee

mouth

eye

hind leg

proboscis

head

antenna

thorax

wing

abdomen

stinger

Words to Know

nectar: a sweet liquid that flowers make

pollen: a yellow powder that flowers make

stingers: pointy body parts that can sting

Read More

Allen, Judy. *Are You a Bee?*
New York: Kingfisher, 2001.

Sexton, Colleen. *Honey Bees.*
Minneapolis: Bellwether Media, 2007.

Websites

Bee Activities and Crafts
http://www.first-school.ws/theme/animals/insects/bee.htm
Choose a bee craft to do. Or print and color bee pictures.

Bee Facts for Kids
http://kids.sandiegozoo.org/animals/insects/bee
Learn more about bees from the San Diego Zoo.

Index